No True Bard

A Selection of the Poems of Ebenezer Elliott

Chosen and edited by Neil Kay

Ebenezer Elliott
1781 - 1849

No True Bard

– A Selection of the Poems of Ebenezer Elliott

Chosen and Edited by Neil Kay

Notes, illustrations and cover copyright © Steven R Kay 2019, 1889books

www.1889books.co.uk

ISBN: 978-1-9996440-7-9

Contents

Publisher's Foreword   i
Introduction   ii

Poems Part 1

1. Sheffield – Town of the Unbowed Poor   1
2. The Country Youth Working in the Town   1
3. The Grinder   2
4. The Poacher of the Manufacturing Districts   3
5. Music still is here   4
6. Saturday   4
7. Lines On the Eleven Poor Men of Hallamshire, Who Originated the Sheffield Political Union.   6
8. From Goethe   7
9. The Death Feast [Part]   7
10. Song – Child, is thy father dead?   8
11. Avarice   9
12. The Patent Parson   9
13. Reform   10
14. Song – New Nap lies at St Helena   11
15. The Jacobin's Prayer [Part]   12
16. Prologue to the Corn Law Rhymes   12
17. Epistle   13
18. The Friendless Muse   14
19. Bard of Our Republic   15
20. Epitaph   16
21. A Poet's Prayer   16
22. Song in Praise of Home-brewed Ale   16

Poems – Part 2

23. [Extracts from] Steam at Sheffield   20
24. Holiday   21

25. Sabbath	22
26. Wonders of the Lane	22
27. The Excursion	24
28. Air and Light on Stanedge	25
29. February	26
30. The Moors – Reflections	26
31. Extracts from The Ranter	28
32. Epigram	30
33. Religion	30
34. Sonnet: Poet vs Parson	31
35. Hymn: Written for the printers of Sheffield	32
36. Hymn: Written for the Rotherham Political Union and Sung There On the Celebration of the	33
37. The Revolution of 1832	34
38. The People's Anthem	34
39. Prayer	35
40. Sonnet On a Pair of Spectacles	36
41. Dreams	36
43. A Poet's Epitaph	37
Appendix 1 – Biographical Note	38
Appendix 2	
1. On poetry	45
2. On Religion	48
Notes	49
Recommended Reading	53
Acknowledgements	54

Foreword

Accessible to the modern reader, this is an introduction to the poetry of Ebenezer Elliott: probably South Yorkshire's most celebrated poet. It should answer the question of all those who walk past his statue in Sheffield's Weston Park and say: "who was he then?"

My dad put this collection together in 2002. I think it was his wish to try to get it published. I am now able to belatedly fulfil that wish.

I have not changed much of his original manuscript. I have added a few pictures and clarified a few points, but that's it. (Oh, and I added poem 22 and gave it a title – I couldn't resist!) If you wish to explore Elliott's poetry in more detail, various e-book versions of the 1876 collection of *The Poetical Works*, and of the *Corn Law Rhymer* are available as well as machine produced digital facsimiles.

This book's title *No True Bard*, comes from his poem entitled *Epistle*, and captures Elliott's self-deprecating humour and defiance.

Historian, Mary Walton wrote in 1948 that Elliott "deserves to be remembered by Sheffield people because he tried to put into words the peculiar emotional reponse of which most lovers of Sheffield are aware: a response to its odd mixture of natural grandeur and man-made squalor, of clanging forges and Cyclopean furnaces and picturesque street names and general drabness relieved by the accidentally attractive groupings of streets and buildings." If this book can go some way to that rememberance it will have achieved its aim.

Steven Kay, 2019

Introduction

Ebenezer Elliott's poetry was popular and widely read during his lifetime, particularly during the 1830s. His *Corn Law Rhymes* were printed in a ninepenny edition by the Sheffield Mechanics Institute and sold thousands. They were read aloud in shops and workshops and declaimed from public platforms. His poetry was also recognised and praised in the established literary journals, by, among others, Thomas Carlyle, who wrote in the *Edinburgh Review* in 1832: "The speaker is of that singular class who has something to say." After his death in 1849 over a thousand people subscribed to a statue, initially erected in Sheffield city centre, but moved to Weston Park in 1875 because it was a nuisance to traffic.

He continued to receive recognition as a poet of merit and maintained a continuing if dwindling readership until the first decade of the twentieth century. During most of the twentieth century academic interest in Britain has been mostly limited to historians addressing his importance in the popular movements of the time, but there have also been recurrent surges of interest in his native South Yorkshire and in the fringe radical press. His poems have been out of print for over a hundred years; though recently an expensive facsimile of the incomplete 1876 edition of his collected works has been published in the USA, where I am informed his reputation is higher than in his own country. I believe that the best of his poetry would be of interest to a wide range of contemporary readers if it was readily available and this has prompted me to put together this small selection.

In the abovementioned *Edinburgh Review* article, Carlyle describes him as "an earnest, truth-seeking man whose great excellence is that he is genuine," a man "who has worked himself loose from cant... into a condition of sincerity." The struggle to achieve this in his poetry was long and difficult. His early poetry was conventional, imitative and stilted. One of these early poems *Night* was described with some justice in the *Atheneaum* as "the ne plus ultra of German horror and bombast." But with some encouragement, and ill-judged advice from the poet Robert Southey, Elliott persisted in writing poetry. He was nearly fifty years old before he found his voice in the three short volumes reviewed by Carlyle. Even here the achievement is uneven. The quality varies according the extent to which his native common sense and passionate concerns lift him out of his reliance on the conventionally "poetical."

For the present day reader it is also off-putting that much of his political poetry deals with issues that now have little interest for non-specialist readers: poems recording and reacting to contemporary events or praising and blaming contemporary politicians. Elliott's passionate and oft-repeated belief that free trade and abolition of taxes on imported grain would by itself be sufficient to lift the poor out of poverty and suffering, now seems at least simplistic, and his angry diatribes against all who oppose this view are repetitive and sometimes tedious. There are too many shrill references to tax-fed worldlings, locustry and bestial powers, and too often the tone is bludgeoning and over-insistent. But his empathy with the sufferings of the poor and his astute and well-crafted descriptions of how the poor respond to, or resist, the oppression and deprivation should hold the interest of many present-day readers. Sometimes his descriptions of dying children and starving widows descend to the mawkish. But not always. Sometimes the depth of feeling and determination to be true to the feeling results in an admirable simplicity. Sometimes, too, he disciplines his anger sufficiently to write incisively in strong but measured tones about their oppressors and those who ignore the plight of the poor.

Elliott also wrote many poems about nature and the local countryside. Some of these remain favourites with a small group of local readers as the poems are concerned with places which are still popular for walking and day excursions. Unfortunately, much of this poetry is marred by use of an over-ornate language such as was still fashionable in the formal poetry of the time through the continuing and pervasive influence of Milton and James Thomson. There are too many "orbs," "dewy bowers," "darting halcyons" and "burning billows." But again, not always. Sometimes he writes with fine observation and a greater degree of linguistic simplicity. In the best of these poems nature is always given a human context and perspective. Visits to the countryside for someone living in early nineteenth century Sheffield, working in industry, were not mere pleasant diversion. They were a vital restorative activity. As Edward Dowden wrote of Elliott in 1911: "The silence and living sounds of the fields and hills bring healing and refreshment to an ear harassed by the din of machinery, the wide and peaceful brightness is a benediction to the eyes smarting from the blear haze of the myriad chimneyed city. Animal refreshment rises by degrees to gratitude, exultation and worship." Many of these poems also gain a wider dimension by being set in a political context, with Elliott championing the "right to roam" against the restrictions of landlords closing commons and footpaths and driving "berrygetters" from the grouse moors. There are poems praising the gentler pleasures of walking in rural lanes and valleys near the city as well as poems celebrating the wildness of the moors. Sometimes in the latter he is able to make positive use of his Miltonic poetic inheritance to convey the sense of grandeur when the changing weather and light over the high hills becomes symbolic of freedom and of powers greater than those of petty despots and oppressors.

He was in his own way a deeply religious man though not a

conventional Christian, and the religious impulse informs and enriches some of his best poetry often arising from the experiences Dowden so aptly describes. In poems such as *The Ranter* he also turns his ire on some of his conventional churchgoing townsmen for their attempt to put constraints on religious expression and experience and for their failure to champion the cause of the poor. But the form and language of much of his poetry owes much to his nonconformist background, to the hymn singing and extempore prayers of the chapels, to the language of sermons and the King James bible. The form and language of some of the shorter poems especially the Corn Law rhymes is also influenced by the lively tradition of popular radical songs which were part o the Sheffield scene during Elliott's life, including the songs of the admirable Joseph Mather who also deserves recognition and reprinting.[1]

Of the formal influences on his poetry, apart from Milton, the most benign is undoubtedly that of his acknowledged master, Geroge Crabbe. In poems such as *The Village Patriarch* and *The Ranter*, Elliott shows he has successfully learned from Crabbe how to break up the metre into a subtle and effective forward and pausing movement used with particular effect in his verse portraits.

This selection includes short poems and extracts from longer poems. The selection is an attempt to present poems which achieve or at least come close to Carlyle's "condition of sincerity," expressed in a voice which has "fashioned itself some clearness." I have therefore excluded poems which I believe fail this test including all the earlier poetry written before *The Village Patriarch* and *The* Corn Law Rhymes. I have, however, included some of the later short poems written after

---

[1] See *Seditious Things: The Songs of Joseph Mather – Sheffield': Georgian Punk Poet*, 1889 Books, 2017

his most productive period. Although in later life the muse of passionately felt poetry seems to have largely deserted him, he was by this time master of his craft of verse and wrote some interesting low-key, short verse on a range of subjects.

The order of the poems bears no relation to the order in which they were written or published. I have put together poems and passages from poems which I think benefit from being read alongside one another, either through similarity or complementarity of theme. Where no title exists I have added one, but these titles are all in Elliott's own words either from the poem itself or in the case of extracts from *The Village Patriarch* from the résumé which precedes each section.

I have divided the poems into two sections:

Part 1. Poems about people living in the poverty, their struggles for dignity or survival, their champions and oppressors – including poems about himself as champion of the oppressed poor.

Part 2. Other poems including poems about the countryside and religion. This includes extracts from two of his better longer poems. The extract from Steam in Sheffield celebrates the steam-powered industry in the city and the extract from *The Ranter* is part of the sermon by the dissident Wesleyan preacher Miles Gordon, which ranges across a number of themes.

Where possible I have used a text approved for publication by Elliott himself, i.e. from the 1832-1835 three volume edition or the two editions entitled *More Verse And Prose* published shortly after his death. This is in preference to using the 1876 two volume collection edited by his son Edwin Elliott in which there are small changes mainly to punctuation and spelling. I have included several poems from the 1876 collection which were omitted from the earlier collection.

I have included 2 appendices:

1) A short account of his life with emphasis on events and reading which influenced the content of the poems in the selection or promotes our understanding of these poems
2) A selection from his prose writings consisting of firstly his views on poetry and poets who have influenced his writing and secondly his views on a range of subjects including religion which have a bearing on some of the poems included in the selection.

Neil Kay, 2002

Poems — Part 1

1. Sheffield – Town of the Unbowed Poor

Ere Bedford's loaf or Erin's sty be thine,
Cloud-rolling Sheffield! want shall humble all.
Town of the unbow'd poor! thou shalt not pine
Like the fall'n rustic, licensed Rapine's thrall,
But, first to rise, wilt be the last to fall!
Slow are thy sons the pauper's trade to learn;
Though, in the land that blossoms like the rose,
The English peasant, and the Irish kerne,
Fight for potatoes, thy proud labourer knows
Nor workhouse wages nor the exile's woes,
Nor yet thy bit of beef, thy pint of ale,
Thy toil – strung heart, which toil could ne'er dismay,
Nor yet thy honest, skill'd right hand shall fail;
Last, from thy hearths the poor man's pride shall stray;
And still shall come thy well-paid Saturday,
And still thy morn of rest be near and sure.

2. The Country Youth Working in the Town

Here oft with fading cheek, and thoughtful brow, Wanders the youth – town-bred, but desert-born,
Too early taught life's deepening woes to know,
He wakes in sorrow with the weeping morn,
And gives much labour for a little corn.
In smoke and dust, from hopeless day to day,
He sweats, to bloat the harpies of the soil,
Who jail no victim, while his pangs can pay.
Untaxing rent, and trebly taxing toil,
They make the labour of his hands their spoil,
And grind him fiercely; but he still can get

A crust of wheaten bread, despite their frowns;
They have not sent him like a pauper yet
For workhouse wages as they send their clowns;
Such tactics do not answer yet, in towns.
Nor have they gorg'd his soul. Thrall though he be
Of brutes who bite him while he feeds them, still
He feels his intellectual dignity,
Works hard, reads usefully, with no mean skill
Writes, and can reason well of good and ill.
He hoards his weekly groat. His tear is shed
For sorrows which his hard-worn hand relieves.
Too poor, too proud, too just, too wise to wed,
[For slaves enough already toil for thieves,]
How gratefully his growing mind receives
The food which tyrants struggle to withhold!
Though hourly ills his every sense invade
Beneath the cloud that o'er his home is roll'd,
He yet respects the power that man hath made,
Nor loathes the despot-humbling sons of trade.
But, when the silent Sabbath-day arrives,
He seeks the cottage, bordering on the moor,
Where still his mother dwells, content, though poor,
And ever glad to meet him at the door.

3. The Grinder

Beautiful rivers of the desert! ye
Bring food for labour from the foodless waste.
Pleas'd stops the wanderer on his way, to see
The frequent weir oppose your heedless haste.
Where toils the Mill, by ancient woods embrac'd,
Hark, how the cold steel screams in hissing fire!
There draws the Grinder his laborious breath;

There, coughing, at his deadly trade he bends;
Born to die young, he fears not man or death;
Scorning the future, what he earns he spends;
Debauch and riot are his bosom friends'
He plays the Tory, sultan-like and well;
Woe to the traitor that dares disobey
The Dey of straps! As rattaned tools shall tell.
Full many a lordly freak, by night, by day,
Illustrates gloriously his lawless sway.
Behold his failings! hath he virtues too?
He is no pauper, blackguard though he be;
Full well he knows what minds combin'd can do'
Full well maintains his birthright. He is free,
And, frown for frown, outstares monopoly,
Yet Abraham and Elliott, both in vain,
Bid science on his cheek prolong the bloom;
He will not live! He seems in haste to gain
The undisturb'd asylum of the tomb,
And, old at two-and-thirty, meets his doom!

4. The Poacher of the Manufacturing Districts

How unlike thee is Jem, the rogue avowed
Whose trade is poaching! Honest Jem works not,
Begs not, but thieves by plundering beggars here.
Wise as a lord, and quite as good a shot,
He, like his betters, lives in hate and fear,
And feeds on partidge, because bread is dear.
Sire of six sons, apprentic'd to the jail,
He prowls in arms, the tory of the night;
With them he shares his battles and his ale;
With him they feel the majesty of might;
No despot better knows that Power is Right.

Mark his unpaidish sneer, his lordly frown;
Hark, how he calls beadle and flunkey liars;
See, how magnificently he breaks down
His neighbour's fence, if so his will requires;
And how his struttle emulates the Squire's!
Jem rises with the moon; But when she sinks, Homeward,
with sack-like pockets and quick heels, Hungry as
boroughmongering ghoul, he slinks.
He reads not, writes not, thinks not – scarcely feels; Insolent
ape! whate'er he gets he steals,
Then plays the devil with his righteous gain!

5. Music still is here

Hark! Music still is here! How wildly sweet
Like flute-notes in a storm, the psalm ascends
From yonder pile, in traffic's dirtiest street!
There hapless woman at her labour bends,
While with the rattling fly her shrill voice blends
And ever, as she cuts the headless nail,
She sings 'I waited long and sought the Lord,
And patiently did bear.' A deeper wail;
Of sister voices joins, in sad accord –
'He set my feet upon his rock ador'd!'
And then perchance – 'O God, on man look down!'

6. Saturday

To-morrow will be Sunday, Ann
Get up, my child, with me;
Thy father rose at four o'clock

To toil for me and thee.

The fine folks use the plates he makes.
And praise it when they dine;
For John has taste – so we'll be neat
Altho' we can't be fine.

Then let us shake the carpet well,
And wash and scour the floor,
And hang the weather-glass he made
Beside the cupboard door.

And polish thou the grate, my love;
I'll mend the sofa arm;
The autumn winds blow damp and chill;
And John loves to be warm

And bring the new white curtain out,
And string the pink tape on –
Mechanics should be neat and clean;
And I'll take heed for John.

And brush the little table, child,
And fetch the ancient books –
John loves to read and when he reads,
How like a king he looks!

And fill the music glasses up
With water fresh and clear;
To-morrow when he sings and plays,
The street will stop to hear.

And throw the dead flowers from the vase
And rub it till it glows;
For in the leafless garden yet
He'll find a winter rose.

And lichen from the wood he'll bring,

And mosses from the dell;
And from the sheltered stubble field
The scarlet pimpernell.

7. Lines On the Eleven Poor Men of Hallamshire, Who Originated the Sheffield Political Union.

Come, drink to the four and the seven.
 Who first bade their breth'ren combine;
Hurra, for the glorious eleven!
 Though their doublets are not very fine.
"Combine, for the wicked conspire!
 Combine!" said the four and the seven;
And Hallam's old eyes darted fire
 At the words of the dreadless eleven.
And what are the four and the seven;
 Whose doublets are not very fine?
And what are the glorious eleven,
 Who first bade the plundered combine?
All useful, all modest, all brave;
 All British through marrow and bone;
There is not among them a slave
 Gold rusted, gold rotten –not one!
Then drink to the four and the seven!
 Though their doublets are not very fine;
The modest and manly eleven,
 Who first bade the plunder'd combine.
"Combine!" said the four and the seven.
 "Combine, for the wicked conspire!"
So spoke the immortal eleven,
 While the eyes of old Hallam flash'd fire.

8. From Goethe

How like a stithy is this land
And we lie on it like good metal
Long hammered by a senseless hand;
But will such thumping make a kettle.

9. The Death Feast [Part]

I bought his coffin with my bed,
  My gown bought earth and prayer;
I pawn'd my mother's ring for bread,
  I pawned my father's chair.
My bible yet remains to sell,
  And yet unsold shall be;
But language fails my woes to tell –
  Even crumbs were scarce with me.
I sold poor Jane's grey linnet then,
  It cost a groat a year;
I sold John's hen, and miss'd the hen
  When eggs were selling dear;
For autumn nights seem'd wintry cold,
  While seldom blazed my fire,
And eight times eight no more I sold
  When eggs were getting higher.
But still I glean the moor and heath
  I wash, they say, with skill;
And workhouse-bread ne'er crossed my teeth.
  I trust it never will.

10. Song – Child, is thy father dead?

[Tune – *Robin Adair*]

Child, is thy father dead?
 Father is gone!
Why did they tax his bread?
 God's will be done!
Mother has sold her bed;
Better to die than wed!
Where shall she lay her head?
 Home have we none!

Father clamm'd thrice a week,
 God's will be done!
Long for work did he seek,
 Work he found none.
Tears on his hollow cheek
Told what no tongue could speak;
Why did his master break?
 God's will be done.

Doctor said air was best,
 Food had we none;
Father, with panting breast,
 Groaned to be gone:
Now he is with the blest –
Mother says death is best!
We have no place of rest
 Yes, ye have one!

11. Avarice

Shall I, lost Britain! Give the pest a name
That, like a cancer, eats into thy core?
Avarice, hungry as devouring flame;
But, swallowing all, it hungers as before,
While flame, its food exhausted, burns no more.
Oh, ye hard hearts, that grind the poor, and crush
Their honest pride, and drink their blood in wine,
And eat their children's bread, without a blush,
Willing to wallow in your pomp, like swine.
Why do ye wear the human form divine?
Can ye make men of brutes contemned, enslav'd?
Can ye grow sweetness on the bitter rue?
Can ye restore the health of minds deprav'd?
And self-esteem in blighted hearts renew?
Why should souls die, to feed such worms as you?
Numidian! who didst say to hated Rome,
'There is no buyer yet to purchase thee!'
Come! from the damn'd of old, Jugurtha come!
See one Rome fall'n! another, mightier, see!
And tell us what the second Rome shall be!
But long, Oh, Heav'n, avert from this sad land
The conflict of the many with the few,
When, crumpled, like a leaf, in havock's hand,
The great, the old, shall vanish from the view,
And slaves be men, all traitors, and all true.

12. The Patent Parson

How like meek Laud, yon Cadi-Dervise scowls!
A patent parson, made to please the Squire!
Priest, Judge, and Jury, for the cure of souls!

Virtues like his no still small voice require;
He cries his wares, and is himself the crier.
No school is built, without his fulsome prayer,
Which fulsome prints, with fulsome praise, record;
No wretch is tried for want, but he is there
In solemn session, sourest on the board,
Where, like Saint Peter, he denies his lord.
O, Cant and Cunning! Mark the contrast well;
The poor, damn'd here, are thankful, though they pine;
Through foul and fair, they limp towards heav'n or hell;
While he, (snug martyr,) when the day is fine,
Seeks Abraham's bosom, and a Tory's wine.
King of bad ale and hares! he shoots, and hunts;
Then whips, or jails, the woe that cannot pay;
Grants Lickgrub's licence, and refuses Grunt's;
Or fines poor Strap, who shaved on Sabbath day;
And like Saint Barebones, he detests a play.

13. Reform

Too long endured, a power and will,
That would be nought, or first in ill,
Has wasted wealth and palsied skill,
    And fed on toil-worn poverty.

They call,d the poor a rope of sand;
And, lo! no rich man's voice or hand
Was raised, throughout the suffering land,
    Against their long iniquity.

They taught the self-rob'd sons of pride
To turn from toil and want aside,
And coin their hearts, guilt petrified,
    To buy a smile from infamy.

They murder'd Hope, they fetteed Trade
The clouds to blood, the sun to shade,
And every good that God had made
    They turn'd to bane and mockery.

They knew no interest, but their own;
They shook the state; they shook the throne;
They shook the world; and God alone
    Seem'd safe in his omnipotence.

Oh, years of crime! The great and true –
The nobly wise – are still the few,
Who bid Truth grow where Falsehood grew,
    And plant it for eternity!

14. Song – Now Nap lies at St Helena

When working blackguards come to blows,
And give or take a bloody nose,
Shall juries try such dogs as those,
    Now Nap lies at St Helena.

No, let the Great Unpaid decide,
Without appeal, on tame bull's hide,
Ash planted well, or fistified,
    Since Nap died at St Helena.

When Sabbath stills the dizzy mill,
Shall Cutler Tom, or Grinder Bill,
On footpaths wander where they will,
    Now Nap lies at St Helena?

No, let them curse, but feel our power;
Dogs! Let them spend their idle hour
Where burns the highway's dusty shower;
    For Nap died at St Helena.

But shall the villains meet and prate
In crowds about affairs of state?
Ride, yeoman, ride! Act, magistrate!
    Nap perish'd at St Helena.

15. The Jacobin's Prayer [Part]

Avenge the plunder'd poor, oh Lord!
But not with fire, but not with sword,
Not as at Peterloo they died
Beneath the hoofs of coward pride.
Avenge our rags, or chains, our sighs,
The famine in our children's eyes!
But not with sword – no, not with fire
Chastise Thou Britain's locustry!
Lord, let them feel thy heavier ire;
Whip them, oh Lord! With poverty!
Then, cold in soul as coffin'd dust,
Their hearts as tearless, dead, and dry,
Let them in outraged mercy trust,
And find that mercy they deny!

16. Prologue to the Corn Law Rhymes

For thee, my county, thee, do I perform
Sternly, the duty of a man born free,

Heedless, though ass, and wolf, and venomous worm,
Shake ears, and fangs, with brandish'd bray, at me;
Alone as Crusoe on th' hostile sea,
For thee, for us, for ours, do I upraise
The standard of my song! For thine and mine,
I toll the knell of England's better days;
And lift my hated voice, that mine and thine
May un-degrade the human form divine.
Perchance, that voice, if heard, is heard too late:
The buried dust of Tyre may wake, and sway
Reconquered seas; but what shall renovate
The dead alive, who dread no judgement day?
Souls, whom the lust of gold hath turn'd to clay?
And what but scorn and slander will reward
The rabble's poet and his honest song?
Gambler for blanks! Thou playest an idiot's card;
For, sure to fall, the weak attack the strong.
Ay, but what strength is theirs, whose might is based on wrong?

17. Epistle

My pious friend! What shall I say
To one so wise and grave?
I got your letter t'other day
It bids me be a slave.

The poor man's joys, the poor man's pain,
You bid my Muse discard;
"Such themes" you say "true bards disdain,"
I, then am no true bard.

Because your dog obeys you well,

And well by you is fed,
Must I obey the dogs of hell
Who growl, and snatch my bread?

Slaves fawn; but do they fawn for nought?
Yes, slaves there are indeed,
Who bribe themselves with their own groat,
And lick the dogs they feed!
A better aim will I prefer
Nor fawn on fool or knave,
Like many a tyrant homager,
Immortal! Yet a slave.

18. The Friendless Muse

But who will listen when the poor complain?
Who read, or hear, a tale of woe, if true?
Ill fares the friendless Muse of want and pain.
Fool! would'st thou prosper, and be honest, too?
Fool! would'st thou prosper? – Flatter those who do.
If, not unmindful of the all-shunned poor,
Thou write on tablets frail their troubles deep,
The proud, the vain, will scorn thy theme obscure.
What wilt thou earn, though lowly hearts may steep
With tears the page in which their sorrows weep?
Growl, if thou wilt, in vulgar sympathy
With plunder'd labour; pour thy honest bile
In satire, hiss'd at base prosperity;
And let his enviers from their pittance vile,
Reward the pauper virtues of thy style.
But, hark! what accents, of what slave, inquire
Why rude mechanics dare to wield the quill?
He bids me from the scribbler's desk retire,

Rehoof my fingers, and forget my skill
In raffling foully, and in writing ill.
Oh, that my poesy were like the child
That gathers daisies from the lap of May,
With prattle sweeter than the bloomy wild!
It then might teach poor wisdom to be gay
As flowers, and birds, and rivers, all at play,
And winds, that make the voiceless clouds of morn
Harmonious. But distemper'd if not mad,
I feed on Nature's bane, and mess with scorn.
I would not, could not, if I would, be glad,
But, like shade-loving plants, am happiest sad.
My heart, once soft as woman's tear, is gnarled
With gloating on the ills I cannot cure.

19. Bard of Our Republic

Oh, Time, is this the island of the just
And the immortal, in her virtues strong?
The land of Shakespeare? Worthy of our dust,
Because she guards the right, and loathes the wrong –
The land of Ireton's bones, and Milton's song?
Rise, Bard of our Republic! – wherefore rise,
Like Samuel to the troubled King of old?
Could'st thou flash living fire in Britons' eyes,
Would pigmy souls be minds of giant mould?

20. Epitaph

Greater than Colon, name renowned
In famed Discovery's rolls,
Here lies Charles Dickens who first found
That poor folk may have souls.

21. A Poet's Prayer

Almighty Father! Let thy lowly child,
Strong in his love of truth, be wisely bold,
A patriot bard, by sycophants revil'd,
Let him live usefully, and not die old!
Let poor men's children, pleas'd to, read his lays,
Love, for his sake, the scenes where he hath been;
And when he ends his pilgrimage of days,
Let him be buried where the grass is green;
Where daisies, blooming earliest, linger late
To hear the bee his busy note prolong
There let him slumber, and in peace await
The dawning morn, far from the sensual throng,
Who scorn the windflower' blush, the red-breast's lonely song.

22. Song in Praise of Home-brewed Ale

Nor alehouse scores, nor alehouse broils
  Turn my good woman pale;
For in my pantry I've a keg
  Of home-brewed ale.
The devil keeps a newspaper
  Where tavern-wranglers rail,

Because it tempts his doomed and lost
    To drink bad ale.
But I read news at second-hand,
    Nor find it flat and stale;
While Hume's or Hindley's health I drink
    In home-brew'd ale.
My boys and girls delight to see
    My friends and me regale,
While Nancy, curtsying, deigns to sip
    Our home-brew'd ale;
And when the widow'd pauper comes,
    To tell her monthly tale,
I sometimes cheer her with a drop
    Of home-brew'd ale;
It tells her heart of better days,
    Ere she grew thin and pale,
When James, before the banker fail'd,
    Drank home-brew'd ale.
I'll melt no money in my drink,
    Where ruffians fight and rail:
The gauger never dipp'd his stick
    In my cheap ale.
But when we household suffrage get,
    And honest men prevail;
Then, hey, mechanics, for free trade,
    And cheaper ale!

Poems – Part 2

23. [Extracts from] Steam at Sheffield

Come, blind old Andrew Turner! Link in mine
Thy time-tried arm, and cross the town with me;
For there are wonders mightier far than thine;
Watt! and his million-feeding enginry!
Thou canst not see, unnumber'd chimneys o'er,
From chimneys tall the smoky cloud aspire;
But thou canst hear the unwearied crash and roar
Of iron powers, that, urg'd by restless fire,
Toil ceaseless, day and night, yet never tire,
Or say to greedy man. "Thou dost amiss."
Oh, there is glorious harmony in this
Tempestuous music of the giant, Steam,
Commingling growl and roar, and stamp and hiss,
With flame and darkness! Like a Cyclops dream,
It stuns our wondering souls, that start and scream
With joy and terror; while, like gold on snow
Is mornings beam on Andrew's hoary hair!

He loves the thunder of machinery!
It is beniticent thunder, though at times,
Like heav'n's red bolt it lightens fatally.
Poor blind old man! What would he give to see
This bloodless Waterloo! This hell of wheels!
This dreadful speed, that seems to sleep and snore,
And dream of earthquake! In his brain he feels
The mighty arm of mist, that shakes the shore
Along the throng'd canal, in ceaseless roar
Urging the heavy forge, the clanking mill,
The rapid tilt, the screaming sparkling stone.

No; there he moves, the thoughtful engineer,
The soul of all this motion; rule in hand,
And coarsely apron'd – simple, plain, sincere –

An honest man; self taught to understand
The useful wonders which he built and plann'd.
Self-taught to read and write – a poor man's son,
Though poor no more – how he would sit alone,
When the hard labour of the day was done,
Bent o'er his table, silent as a stone,
To make the wisdom of the wise his own!
How oft' of Brindley's deeds th'apprenticed boy
Would speak delighted, long ere freedom came!
And talk of Watt! While shedding tears of joy,
His widow'd mother heard, and hoped the name
Of her poor boy, like heirs would rise to fame.

24. Holiday

O blessed ! when some holiday
   Brings townsmen to the moor,
And, in the sunbeams, brighten up
   The sad looks of the poor.
The bee puts on his richest gold,
   As if that worker knew
How hardly [and for little] they
   Their sunless task pursue.
But from their souls the sense of wrong
   On dove-like pinion flies;
And, throned o'er all, Forgiveness sees
   His image in their eyes
Soon tired, the street born lad lies down
   On marjoram and thyme,
And through his grated finger sees
   The falcon's flight sublime;
Then his pale eyes, so bluely dull,
   Grow darkly blue with light,

And his lips redden like the bloom
   O'er miles of mountain bright.
The little lovely maiden-hair
   Turns up its happy face,
And saith unto the poor man's heart
   "Thou'rt welcome to this place."

25. Sabbath

Hail! Sabbath! day of mercy, peace, and rest!
That o'er loud cities throws't a noiseless spell,
The hammer there, the wheel, the saw, molest
Pale thought no more. O'er trades contentious hell
Meek quiet spreads her wings invisible.
But, when thou com'st, less silent are the fields
Through whose sweet paths the toil-freed towns-man steals.
To him the very air a banquet yields.
Envious, he watches the poised hawk, that wheels
His flight on chainless winds. Each cloud reveals
A paradise of beauty to his eye.

26. Wonders of the Lane

Strong climber of the mountain's side
   Though thou the vale disdain,
Yet walk with me where hawthorns hide
   The wonders of the lane.
High o'er the rushy springs of Don
   The stormy gloom is roll'd;
The moorland hath not yet put on
   His purple, green, and gold.

But here the titling spreads his wing,
  Where dewy daisys gleam;
And here the sun flower of the spring
  Burns bright in morning's beam.
To mountain winds the famished fox
  Complains that Sol is slow,
O'er headlong steeps and gushing rocks
  His royal robe to throw.
But here the lizard seeks the sun,
  Here coils in light the snake;
And here the firetuft hath begun
  Its beauteous nest to make.
Oh, then, while hums the earliest bee
  Where verdure fires the plain,
Walk thou with me, and stoop to see
  The glories of the lane!
For, oh, I love these banks of rock,
  This roof of sky and tree,
These tufts, where sleeps the gloaming clock,
  And wakes the earliest bee!
As spirits from eternal day
  Look down on earth secure;
Gaze thou, and wonder, and survey
  A world in miniature;
  A world not scorn'd by Him who made
  Even weakness by his might;
But solemn in his depth of shade,
  And splendid in his light.
Light! not alone on clouds afar
  O'er storm-loved mountains spread,
Or widely teaching sun and star
  Thy glorious thoughts are read;
Oh, no! thou art a wond'rous book,
  To sky and sea, and land
A page on which the angels look,

    Which insects understand!
And here, oh, Light! minutely fair,
    Divinely plain and clear,
Like splinters of a chrystal hair,
    A bright small hand is here.

27. The Excursion

Bone-weary, many-childed, trouble-tried!
Wife of my bosom, wedded to my soul!
Mother of nine that live, and two that died!
This day, drink health from Nature's mountain bowl.
Nay, why lament the doom which mocks control?
The buried are not lost, but gone before.
Then dry thy tears, and see the river roll
O'er rocks, that crown'd yon time-dark heights of yore,
Now, tyrant- like , dethroned, to crush the weak no more.

The young are with us yet, and we with them:
Oh, thank the Lord for all he gives and takes –
The withered bud, the living flower, or gem!
And he will bless us, when the world forsakes!
Lo, where thy fisher-born, abstracted, takes
With his fix'd eyes, the trout he cannot see!
Lo, starting from his earnest dream, he wakes!
While our glad Fanny, with rais'd foot and knee,
Bears down at Noe's side, the bloom-bow'd hawthorn tree.

Dear children! When the flowers are full of bees;
When sun-touched blossoms shed their fragrant snow;
When song speaks like a spirit, from the trees
Whose kindled greenness hath a golden glow;
When, clear as music, rill and river flow,

With trembling hues, all changeful, tinted o'er
By that bright pencil which good spirits know
Alike in earth and heaven; 'tis sweet once more,
Above the sky-tinged hills to see the storm-bird soar.

'Tis passing sweet to wander, free as air,
Blythe truants in the bright and breeze-bless'd da
Far from the town – where stoop the sons of care
O'er plans of mischief, till their souls turn grey,
And dry as dust, and dead-alive are they,
Of all self buried things the most unbless'd;
Oh, Morn, to them no blissful tribute pay!
Oh, Night's long-courted slumbers! bring no rest
To men who laud man's foes, and deem the basest best!

God! would they handcuff thee? And if they could,
Chain the free air, that like the daisy, goes
To every field; and bid the warbling wood
Exchange no music with the willing rose
For love-sweet odours, where the woodbine blows
And trades with every cloud, and every beam
Of the rich sky! Their gods are bonds and blows,

Rocks and blind Shipwreck; and they hate the stream
That leaves them all behind, and mocks their changeless dream.

28. Air and Light on Stanedge

Air! Vital Air! And beauty-breathing light!
The acred demons have not tax'd you here,
As in the dim town's thick blood-thickening night
Of nights and days, where men from year to year

Toil for restricted food. Twins! pure and bright
As sister angels, clad in stainless white!
Free dwell ye on the mountain's summit bare:
And man shall yet be free, in hell's despite,
To reap enfranchised harvests everywhere;
Nor want ask leave to toil, law-wedded to despair.

29. February

Rivers are torrents, vales and plains are lakes,
When February draws her curtains down.
Rain! Rain! The universal snow forsakes
Moorland and mountain, forest, farm, and town.
Rain! Rain! It pours, it pours. Red land-floods drown Blue
ocean's baffled tide. With calm cold frown,
The cold grey rock, that saw death's cradle, wakes
From his old dream of drowth, to find his home
In cloud-hung deluge. The old forest shakes
His wrinkled forehead o'er the whirling foam
Of inland sea; and with a haste that takes
Life's sad last blessing, down the revels come
Of sky and upland, mix'd in cataract
That rioteth in waste, like one who long hath lack' d.

30. The Moors – Reflections

Father, we stand upon the mountain stern
That cannot feel our lightness, and disdains
Reptiles that sting and perish, in their turn,
That hiss and die – and lo, no trace remains
Of all their joys, their triumphs, and their pains!

Yet to stand here might well exalt the mind:
These are not common moments, nor is this
A common scene. Hark, how the coming wind
Booms, like the funeral dirge of woe, and bliss,
And life, and form, and mind, and all that is!
How like the wafture of a world-wide wing
It sounds and sinks and all is hush'd again!
But are our spirits humbled? No! We string
The lyre of death with mystery and pain,
And proudly hear the dreadful notes complain
That man is not the whirlwind, but the leaf,
Torn from the tree to soar and disappear.
Grand is our weakness, and sublime our grief.
Lo, on this rock, I shake off hope and fear,
And stand releas'd from clay! Yet am I here,
And at my side are blindness, age and woe.
Hail, silence of the desert! – I speak low
In reverence. Here the falcon's wing is aw'd,
As o'er the deep repose, sublimely slow,
He wheels in conscious majesty abroad.
Spirits should make the desert their abode.
The meekest, purest, mightiest, that e'er wore
Dust as a garment, stole from crowds unbless'd
To sea-like forests, or the sea-beat shore,
And utter'd, on the star sought mountain's breast,
The holiest precepts e'er to dust address'd.
Oh, happy, souls of death-freed men, if here
Ye wander in your noiseless forms unseen!
Though not remote, removed from grief and fear,
And, all that pride shall be, and guilt hath been;
While gentle death his shadow casts between
Thoughts seraph-wing'd, and man's infirmity.

31. Extracts from The Ranter

"God blames not him who toils six days in seven,
Where smoke and dust bedim the golden day,
If he delight, beneath the dome of heaven,
To hear the winds, or see the clouds at play,
Or climb His hills, amid their flowers to pray.
Ask ye, if I, of Wesley's followers one,
Abjure the house where Wesleyans bend the knee?
I do – because the spirit thence is gone;
And truth, and faith, and grace, are not, with me,
The Hundred Popes of England's Jesuitry.
We hate not the religion of bare walls;
We scorn not the cathedral'd pomp and prayer;
For sweet are all our father's festivals,
If contrite hearts the heavenly banquet share,
In field or temple: God is everywhere!

Pious they are, cool, circumspect, severe;
And while they feel for woes beyond the wave,
They laud the tyrants who starve millions here:
The famish'd Briton must be fool or knave,
But wrongs are precious in a foreign slave.
Their Bibles for the heathen load our fleets;
Lo, gloating eastward, they inquire, 'What news?'
We die, we answer, foodless in the streets!
And what reply your men of Gospel-views?
On, they are sending bacon to the Jews!
Their lofty souls have telescopic eyes,
Which see the smallest speck of distant pain,
While at their feet, a world of agonies,
Unseen, unheard, unheeded, writhes in vain.

Oh, for a Saint, like those who sought and found,
For conscience' sake, sad homes beyond the main!

The Fathers of New England, who unbound,
In wild Columbia, Europe's double chain;
The men whose dust cries 'Sparta, live again!'
The slandered Calvinists of Charles's time
Fought, and they won it, Freedom's holy fight.
With zeal they preach' d, with reverence they were heard;
For in their ring creed, sublime, sincere,
Danger was found, that parson-hated word!
They flatter'd none – they knew nor hate nor fear.
But taught the will of God and did it here.

O for a ship – a ship! – the wing of steam
To bear us from the land, where toil despised
Is robbed and scourged, and life's best prospects seem
Sad as the couch of patience agonized!
Is there no land where useful men are prized
By those they feed? Or will there never be
For hope a refuge, and a dwelling place
Where tyrants, in their mad rapacity,
Shake not their clench'd fists in the Almighty's face,
And cry "Thou fool!" Shall glorious seas embrace
A thousand shores in vain? Shall paupers grow,
Where HE hath said the eagle's young shall feed?
Shall hopeless tears to water deserts flow,
While flow his mighty streams, with none to heed,
And make fertility a baneful weed?

Poor bread-tax'd slaves, have ye no hope on earth?
Yes, God from evil still educes good;
Sublime events are rushing to their birth;
Lo, tyrants by their victims are with stood!
And Freedom's seed still grows, though steep'd in blood!
When, by our Father's voice the skies are riven,
That, like the winnowed chaff, disease may fly;
And seas are shaken by the breath of heaven,

Lest in their depth the living spirit die;
Man views the scene with awed but grateful eye,
And trembling feels, could God abuse his power,
Nor man, nor nature, would endure an hour.
But there is mercy in his seeming wrath;
It smites to save, not tyrant-like, to slay;
And storms have beauty, as the lily hath:
Grand are the clouds that mirror'd on the bay,
Roll like the shadows of lost worlds away,
When bursts through broken gloom the startled light;
Grand are the waves, that like that broken gloom,
Are smitten into splendour by His might;
And glorious is the storm's tremendous boom,
Although it waileth o'er a watery tomb,
And is a dreadful ode on ocean's drown'd.

32. Epigram

"Man! Put no trust in mysteries
   Which none can understand
Such dreams have sown iniquities
        O'er every land
Dream not, but work! That Love and Peace
   May o'er all states preside."
These words "thy wisest" spoke, oh Greece,
        And therefore died.

33. Religion

What is Religion? "Speak the truth in love."
Reject no good. Mend if thou canst, thy lot.

Doubting, enquire, – nor dictate till thou prove.
Enjoy thy own – exceed not, trespass not.
Pity the scorners of life's meanest thing.
If wrong'd, forgive – that hate may lose its sting.
Think, speak, work, get – bestow, or wisely keep,
So live, that thou may'st smile and no one weep.
So bless'd – like birds, that sing because they love:
And bless – like rivers singing to the sun,
Giving and taking blessings, as they run:
Or soft-voic'd showers, that cool the answering grove,
When cloudy wings are wide in heav'n display'd,
And blessings brighten o'er the freshen'd sod,
Till earth is like the countenance of God.
This is Religion! saith the bard of trade.

34. Sonnet: Poet vs Parson

A hireling's wages to the priest are paid;
While lives and dies, in want and rags, the bard!
But preaching ought to be its own reward,
And not a sordid, if an honest trade.
Paul, labouring proudly with his hands, arrayed
Regenerated hearts in peace and love;
And when, with power, they preached the mystic dove,
Penn, Barclay, Clarkson, asked not Mammon's aid.
As, for its own sake, poetry is sweet
To poets – so, on tasks of mercy bound,
Religion travels with unsandaled feet,
Making the flinty desert holy ground;
And never will her triumph be complete
While one paid pilgrim upon earth is found.

35. Hymn: Written for the printers of Sheffield

Lord! taught by Thee, when Caxton bade
  His silent words for ever speak;
A grave for tyrants then was made,
  Then crack'd the chain which yet shall break.

For bread, for bread, the all-scorn'd man,
  With study worn, his press prepared;
And knew not Lord, thy wondrous plan,
  Nor what he did, nor what he dar'd.

When first the might of deathless thought
  Impress'd his all- instructing page,
Unconscious giant! How he smote
  The fraud and force of many an age!

The pow'r he grasp'd let none disdain;
  It conquered once, and conquers still;
By fraud and force assail'd in vain,
  It conquer'd erst, and ever will.

It conquers here! The fight is won!
  We thank thee, Lord, with many a tear!
For many a not unworthy son
  Of Caxton, does thy bidding here.

We help ourselves, thy cause we aid;
  We build for Heav'n, beneath the skies:
And bless thee, Lord, that thou hast made
  Our daily bread of tyrants' sighs.

36. Hymn: Written for the Rotherham Political Union and Sung There On the Celebration of the Passing of the Three Reform Bills

We thank thee Lord of Earth and heav'n
For hope and strength and triumph given!
We thank thee that our fight is won,
Although our work is but begun.

We met, we crushed the evil powers;
A nobler task must now be ours –
Their victims maim'd and poor to feed,
And bind the bruised and broken reed.

Oh, let not Ruin's will be done,
When Freedom's fight is fought and won!
The deed of Brougham, Russell, Grey,
Outlives the night! Lord, give us day!

Grant time, grant patience, to renew,
What England's foes and thine o'erthrew:
If they destroyed, let us restore,
And say to misery, mourn no more.

Lord, let the human storm be still'd!
Lord, let the million moths be fill'd!
Let labour cease to toil in vain!
Let England be herself again!

Then shall this land her arms stretch forth,
To bless the East, and tame he North;
On tyrant's hearths wake buried souls,
And call to life the murdered Poles.

Sing, Britons, sing! the sound shall go

Wherever England finds a foe;
This day a trumpet's voice is blown
O'er every despot's heart and throne.

37. The Revolution of 1832

See, the slow Angel writhes in dreams of pain!
    His cheek indignant glows!
Like Stanedge, shaking thunder from his mane,
    He starts from his repose.
Wide, wide, his earthquake voice is felt and heard:
    "Arise, ye brave and just!"
The living sea is to its centre stirr'd –
    And, lo! our foes are dust!
The earth beneath the feet of millions quakes;
    The whirlwind cloud is riv'n;
As midnight smitten into lightning, wakes,
    So wak'd the sword of Heav'n.
The angel drew not from its sheath that sword;
    He spake and all was done!
Night fled away before the Almighty word,
    And lo! the sun! the sun!

38. The People's Anthem

When wilt thou save the people?
  Oh. God of Mercy! When?
Not kings and lords, but nations!
  Not thrones and crowns, but men!
Flowers of thy heart, oh, God, are they!
Let them not pass, like weeds, away!

Their heritage a sunless day!
> God, save the people!

Shall crime bring crime for ever.
  Strength aiding still the strong?
Is it thy will, oh, Father,
  That man shall toil for wrong?
"No!" say thy mountains; "No!" thy skies;
"Man's clouded sun shall brightly rise,
And songs be heard, instead of sighs."
> God, save the people!

When wilt thou save the people?
  Oh, God of Mercy! When?
The people, Lord, the people!
  Not thrones and crowns, but men!
God! save the people! thine they are,
Thy children, as thy angels fair:
Save them from bondage, and despair!
> God! save the people!

39. Prayer

Lord! Grant to poor o'er laboured man
More leisure and less prayer,
More church, less priest – and homes for inns!
More libraries, and fewer sins;
More music and less care.

40. Sonnet On a Pair of Spectacles

How many men, who liv'd to bless mankind,
Have died unthank'd! Far teaching and self taught,
They did what learning scorns to learn or teach;
Their deeds are portion of the general thought;
Their thoughts have pass'd into the common speech,
And labour's wages: yet they left behind
No name, nor record! save the good which grew
Out of the sacrifice that gives and saves.
Lo, what a tree is rising from their graves,
To shelter ev'n on earth, the wise and true!
Then, worship not fam'd words, which, like the winds,
Or Homer's song, seem things that cannot die,
And ever lived; they are but names of minds
When good or evil speaks immortally.

41. Dreams

Dreams! Are ye vapours of the heated brain
Or echoes of our deeds, our fears, our hopes?
Fever'd remembrances that o'er again
Tell prose adventures, in poetic tropes,
While drowsy judgement with illusion copes
Feebly and vainly? Are ye paid when due?
Or like our cobweb wealth, unfound when sought?
Be ye of sterling value, weigh'd and true,
Or the mere paper currency of thought
By spendthrift fancy signed, and good for nought.

43. A Poet's Epitaph

Stop. Mortal! Here thy brother lies,
  The Poet of the Poor
His books were rivers, woods and skies,
  The meadow and the moor;
His teachers were the torn hearts wail,
  The tyrant, and the slave,
The street, the factory, and the jail,
  The palace – and the grave!

Appendix 1 – Biographical Note

Ebenezer Elliott was one of a family of eleven was born at Masbrough, Rotherham in 1781. His birth was not registered anywhere except in the family bible. His father who moved from Newcastle worked as a clerk in an iron foundry having been given what is described as a good commercial education by his own father, a Newcastle whitesmith. His grandmother was a Scotswoman and his mother was 'a daughter of a yeoman' from a village near Penistone.

Much of the information about Ebenezer's forbears and childhood comes from his own memoirs and there is a suggestion that he may have at the least been prone to selectivity and exaggeration, embroidering the facts in order to convey a desired message. In different memoirs he describes himself as a having descended from "respectables" and from "border thieves who lived on cattle they stole from the English and the Scotch."

He describes his father as an ultra calvinist and extreme radical, preaching on hell 'hung round with span long children' and repeatedly declaiming on the virtues of Cromwell and Washington. For many years Ebenezer Elliott senior was known as Devil Elliott by 'those who hated the poor and honoured the king.' He is said to have attacked a fully armed cavalry officer with a stick when the latter deliberately backed his horse into his shop window and on another occasion he used the same stick to fight four robbers who attacked him when walking home killing one before being knocked unconscious himself Ebenezer junior wrote of him in one on his memoirs "From his first to his last gasp I doubt whether he knew what it was to be afraid, except of poverty..."

There is little known about Elliott's early upbringing by this formidable man, though it would be easy to speculate about how this shaped his own character and attitudes. One incident from his early childhood is recorded, an account of how his father used to bath his children in the canal immersing them three times and on the final immersion held them under for several seconds which Ebenezer says gave him a lasting fear of suffocation.

Ebenezer writes that he was closer to his mother, a gentle and warm hearted woman with chronic ill health and this presumably fostered the compassionate and caring side of his character. But he nevertheless held to many of his father's attitudes and values, writing in later life that he had retained his political integrity "without abjuring one article of my father's fearless creed." His religious views as demonstrated in his poetry were nevertheless very different from his father's though it is suggested by one biographer that Elliott Senior also ameliorated his religious extremism in later life and may even have become something of a sceptic.

The young Ebenezer was sent to several successive schools but says he was a dull scholar and learned little more from his formal education than to write. He says that his lack of success and adverse comparisons with his brother Giles "threw a shade of sadness over a nature dull and slow, but thoughtful and affectionate." Because of his lack of success at school and habitual truancy he was left to his own devices for long periods during his childhood and spent many days playing alone by the canal. He writes that as a child he was "always alone and that this is perhaps why I was deemed lacking in intellect." but adds that his solitude was not unhappy as he was the best maker of kites and model ships in the district and spent his time delightfully swimming his little fleet of ships and repairing his fortresses on the banks of the canal between the Greasborough and Rawmarsh bridges. After such excursions he writes that on his return "I trembled when I neared home for I knew not how to answer the questions which I feared my father would put to me. Sometimes I avoided them by slinking to bed after supper."

He was proud that like Burns he was self-educated. One of the first books to capture his interest was his aunt's copy of *Sowerby's English Botany*. Encouraged by this aunt he learned to copy the illustrations and went on to collect and draw plants from life. At the age of 9 he began to neglect chapel attendance preferring to spend his Sundays gathering flowers to draw. When he was 14 a clergyman from North Yorkshire bequeathed his father a collection of several hundred books, which included Shenstone's poems. Young's *Night Thoughts*, Shakespeare, Milton and Tom Paine's *Common Sense*. Ebenezer had full access to these books. By the age of 12 he claims he could recite without missing a word, books 1, 2 and 6 of *Paradise Lost* and that by 16 he knew most of the bible by heart. Although he says he could never learn rules of grammar he says he learned to write English as correctly as Samuel Johnson by studying the best examples and by correcting his own writing through reflection and perseverance.

According to his biographer, John Watkins, his father, despairing of his lack of success at school decided that he was unfit for anything other than manual work and at the age of 16 put him to work at the foundry alongside rough and uneducated working men. Elliott himself comments that that far from being punishment work at the foundry released him from a sense of inferiority which had long depressed him for he was found to be no less clever than other beginners. He also remembers without resentment the time he spent listening to the "plain or coarse and sometimes brutal, but more often instructive and pathetic conversations of workmen." At this time also he says he could play his part "at the York Keelman public house with the best of its customers," but adds that he never thoroughly relished the course enjoyments of the alehouse as his thoughts continually wandered to the canal banks. Also his interest in botany and poetry continued to grow. On the flyleaf of his copy of *Thomson's Seasons* he wrote in 1834 "I suspect that this is the very book that weaned me from the alehouse and made a rhymer of me."

From 1797 to 1804 he worked for his father for no more than a little pocket money. Later his father's views of his son's commercial abilities must have changed for he took him into partnership along with his brother Giles. He married Fanny Gartside believed to be the daughter of a shopkeeper selling hosiery and hats on Rotherham High street in 1805. Ebenezer eventually bought out his father and brother part with his wife's capital and part with a mortgage but this overstretched him financially and his difficulties were compounded by the downturn in trade after the end of the Napoleonic wars. The business failed in 1819 and Ebenezer lost his house as well as his source of income. It is said that he was saved from complete ruin by a gift of money from Earl Fitzwilliam who knew of his poetry. After the collapse of his business Ebenezer and his family lived for a time with his mother's maiden sisters. He describes this as a time of personal depression when he even thought about suicide. Borrowed capital of £150 mainly from his wife's sisters enabled him to restart in business, supplying materials for the cutlery trade and for this purpose he moved to live in neighbouring Sheffield. He already had 9 children at this stage in his life and the whole family moved to their new home in a cart. He lived at Upperthorpe, which was then a leafy village on the outskirts, from 1834 to 1841. The house is still there and has a blue plaque. (If your brakes failed going down Blake Street you'd crash into it.)

E.P Thompson describes Sheffield at this time as a comparatively prosperous town with a high proportion of skilled artisans – both small masters and wage earning craftsmen. Ebenezer himself writes of the many thousands of intelligent operatives working in the town. Following the move he prospered in business for the next 18 years. He also found his individual voice in poetry during his Sheffield years as well as becoming active in the political life of the town. He was one of the very few members of the employer class who joined with working men in developing such bodies as the Sheffield Anti Bread Tax Society, the Sheffield Political Union and the Chartists. He was a delegate from Sheffield to the big public meeting the Chartists held at Palace Yard, Westminster in 1838 and stood bail for the Chartist Leader Foden in 1839, losing his bond when Foden absconded. Paul Rogers, Secretary of the Sheffield Mechanics Institute pays tribute to the way Elliott supported their project writing and speaking for them as well as assisting financially. Later in 1839 he withdrew support from several of these bodies when he perceived that the demagogues, such as Samuel Holberry, were getting the upper hand and use of physical force became "the order of the day." In the case of the Chartists his decision to dissociate himself was also partly consequent on their changing their stance on Corn Law repeal.

It was inevitable that he should make some enemies among the Sheffield middle classes by his support for working class protest. In the first election after the 1832 Reform Act Elliott proposed the radical candidate and addressed an assembled crowd said to number 30,000, reciting one of his poems. In the riots which followed the failure of either of the radicals to secure election, 5 men were killed when the infantry were ordered to fire on the crowd and Elliott was blamed for inciting the trouble. The description of Methodists in poems such as *The Ranter* and the savage attacks on established power in the *Corn Law Rhymes* also must have alienated influential people in the city. His treatment of some people who came to his shop must have had the same effect. In 1852, January Searle who edited his memoirs describes how he drove a "semi-clerical gentleman" out of his shop shouting "Away with you! Do my friends come here to be insulted by you…" In 1839 his application to join the Sheffield Literary and Philosophical Society was refused and he claims that he narrowly avoided being expelled from the Public Library for bringing a copy of *Boccaccio's Decameron* onto the premises. It is also recorded that the Attorney General's Office considered prosecuting him for encouraging sedition at one stage but that no proceedings were instituted.

Further children were born to the Elliotts during these Sheffield years. Little is known of his wife but she was evidently an educated, or self-educated, woman with an independent mind who shared his interest in books though not his interest in walking in the countryside. Of their thirteen children five died during childhood.

In 1837 he suffered further business reverses alongside many other Sheffield manufacturers. He states that he lost a third of his savings over the following four years. However, after "enabling 6 boys leave the nest" he was able to retire in 1841 with savings of £6000. On retirement he moved to Great Houghton a village near Barnsley with his wife and daughters building an 8 roomed cottage on 10 acres of land he had purchased. He devoted much of his time at Great Houghton to improving and running his small estate and to extensive reading including Pascal and Spinoza. He wrote and published relatively little over the next 8 years, also declining various offers to take part in public affairs, giving the excuse of age. He died at Great Houghton in 1849, and is buried in the churchyard in Darfield.

Elliott's grave in Darfield

Chronology of publication of poetry

[This sets out first publication dates of poetry in book form, though many poems first appeared in pamphlets, journals etc.]
1818 Night
1823 Love, The Giaour
1829 The Village Patriarch
1830 The Ranter
1831 Corn Law Rhymes
1833 Poetical Works volume 1
1834 Poetical Works Volume 2
1835 Poetical works Volume 3 [Includes *Steam at Sheffield, The Excursion, Corn Law Hymns*]
1850 More Verse and Prose Volumes 1 & 2
1872 Collected Poems edited by Edwin Elliott [Contains some poems previously not published in book form]

Appendix 2

1. On poetry

From a Lecture on the Principle that Poetry is Self Communion - Written for the Hull Mechanics Institute:

I may be wrong in my opinions on ...poetry, but I have endeavoured to be right; and what I say to you on this occasion is my own, or made such by reflection, for I take no mans opinion on trust.

If I tell you anything about poetry, but what you have already felt to be true, I am unfit to address you on the subject: for what is poetry- what can it be — but the heart speaking to itself The principle of earnest self communion — on which all composition purporting to be poetry must stand, or wanting it, fall — I now purpose to elucidate by examples.

When a poet, ceasing to commune with himself, addresses others, he may be eloquent, but he is no longer poetical.

Poetry then, is sincerity, in earnest – impassioned truth – the heart not the head speaking to itself.

Poetry like truth is a common flower. God has sown it over the earth like daisies. [...] Wherever there are hearts that feel it can be found – in the budding rose, and the fading leaf, in the palace and the cottage, in the workshop and the jail.

And then, if any true-hearted man tells you that he does not understand poetry, tell him, in reply, that it is the business of his life, that he practises it every day. "For wisdom lives with children round her knees."

He who compels or willingly suffers a human being to remain in ignorance, does much worse than throw away a man; he converts a man into a beast, fit only to beget creatures destined to live and perish miserably – creatures without minds and therefore not men!"

From A Lecture on Cowper and Burns – Written for the Sheffield Mechanics Institute

Burns, however, had a great advantage over Cowper, in his option of rhyming either in English or his sweet native Doric… For Burns was not the prototype of the truthfulness of Scottish song, the ancient minstrels of Scotland did not forget to avail themselves of the marvellous facilities which the dialect of their country affords to the poet; but Burns has excelled their best productions.

From The Atheneaum Autibiographical Memoir

I never felt any respect for the patrons of inspired milkmaids and ploughmen, for milkmaids and ploughmen if inspired cannot long need patronage, but I knew that, unwilling to believe aught good of the poor, the rich, when a poor man's deeds shames theirs, transform the individual into a marvel at the expense of his class, because being wronged, they hate it.

I cannot, like Byron or Montgomery, pour poetry from the heart as from an unfailing fountain. My thoughts are all exterior, my mind is the mind of my eyes. A primrose is to me a primrose and nothing more. I love it because it is nothing more. There is not in my writing one good idea that has not been suggested to me by some real occurrence, or by some object actually before my eyes or by thoughts of men heard or read.

From the Preface to *The Village Patriarch*

I might truly be called an unfortunate imitator of Crabbe, that most British of poets; for he has long been bosomed with me; and if he had never lived, it is possible that I might never have written pauper poetry. [...] The clerical artist works with a wire brush; but he has been unjustly blamed for the stern colours in which he paints the sublimity of British wretchedness. [...] Wordsworth has coloured similar objects differently! True, but Wordsworth only meets his subject half-way, and with his hinder end towards it. [...] Crabbe, on the contrary, takes his hideous mistress in his arms, and she rewards his confidence in her, by telling him all her dreadful secrets. The severity of his style is an accident, belonging, not to him, but the majesty of his unparalleled subject.

From a letter to Ebenezer Hingston 1843 [Printed in John Watkins biography]

Verse is not poetry. It must be essentially antipoetical if it restrains the free expression of feeling Shakespeare and Milton rejected rhyme for blank verse and Scott both for prose.

2. On Religion

From a letter to John Watkins 1844

Why should there be more than one church – that which every good man carries within his heart of hearts. I am opposed to all paid preaching. The Methodists could, and I believe would, alone and unassisted, have brought down the Corn Laws, if they had had no paid preachers.

From the Commonplace Book kept during his retirement at Great Houghton.

Jesus was simply a man approved of by God.

Scorn no religion, not even that of the savage, for in him too is the deep feeling of the unknown mystery in which we live and die.

Notes

1. Sheffield – Town of the Unbowed Poor. From *The Village Patiarch* book III
- Bedford's loaf. A reference to the practice of topping up agricultural low wages with Poor Law Payments known as the Speenhamland system, widespread in southern counties
- Erin. An ancient and literary word for Ireland.
- Kerne. An Irish countryman.

2. The Country Youth Working in the Town. From *The Village Patriarch* book III
- desert born. desert is used with the earlier meaning of any uncultivated tract of country i.e the moorland.
- workhouse wages. See note above on Speenhamland system.

3. The Grinder. From *The Village Patriarch* book V
- Dey of straps. The Dey was the autocratic commandant of an elite section of the Turkish army. An elaborate system of straps connected the grindstones to the water wheel which powered the grinding process.
- rattaned tools. Rattaning was the practice of removing and hiding tools to enforce compliance to the collective will of a group of workers
- Abraham and Elliott. Inventors of a device to remove the noxious dust generated in the grinding process. Grinders were said to be reluctant to use the device allegedly on the grounds that any lowering of the death rate would result in surplus labour and lower wages.

4. The Poacher. From *The Village Patriarch* book III
- unlike thee. i.e. unlike the artisan, referring back to the previous section
- beadle an officer of the magistrates court
- boroughmongering. Refers to the practice of selling parliamentary seats in the unreformed parliament.
- struttle. Strutting [dialect?]

5. Music still is here. From *The Village Patriarch* book I

6. Saturday. From *Poetical Works* 1876 Edited by Edwin Elliott

7. Lines on the Eleven Poor Men of Hallamshire. From *Corn Law Rhymes*

8. From Goethe. From *Poetical Works* Vol 3 1835
- stithy. Anvil [dialect]

9. The Death Feast. From *Corn Law Rhymes*

10. Song. Child, is thy father dead? From *Corn Law Rhymes*
- clamm'd. Starving [dialect]

11. Avarice. From *The Village Patriarch* book IX Numidian/Jugurtha.. Jugurtha, king of the Numidians, a North African Tribe fought the Romans in the 2nd century BCE.

12. The Patent Parson. From *The Village Patriarch* book VII
- Laud. Archbishop and supporter of Charles 1sts personal rule prior to the English Revolution
- Abraham's bosom – land of the blessed dead c.f. Luke, 16,22.
- Saint Barebones. A nickname for a 17th century anabaptist preacher opposed to the restoration of the monarchy and the reopening of theatres.
- Cadi-dervise – a Cadi is a judge in a muslim community, and Dervise is an old spelling of Dervish - a Turkish or Persian monk, especially one who professes extreme poverty and leads an austere life.

13. Reform. From *Corn Law Rhymes*

14. Song. Now Nap lies at St Helena. From *Corn Law Rhymes*. Elliott continued to see Napoleon as a champion of the poor [albeit flawed] and displayed his bust alongside busts of Ajax and Achilles in his Sheffield workshop.

15. The Jacobin's Prayer. From *Corn Law Rhymes*
- Jacobin. The term was used for all people committed to uncompromising egalitarian principles, English as well as French.

16. Prologue to the Corn Law Rhymes. From *Poetical Works* Vol 3 1835
- Tyre reconquered seas – The Phoenicians of ancient Tyre were great seamen and traders
- Blanks – discs of metal prior to stamping i.e. of little worth.

17. Epistle. From *Poetical Works* Vol 3 1835

18. The Friendless Muse. From *The Village Patriarch* book III.

19. Bard of our Republic. From *The Village Patriarch* book VII
- Bard – Milton
- Ireton – a general in Cromwell's army

20. Epitaph From *Poetical Works* 1876 Edited Edwin Elliott
- Colon – Christopher Columbus

21. A Poet's Prayer. From *Corn Law Rhymes* windflower – the wood anemone.

22. Song in Praise of Home-brewed Ale. From *Poetical Works* 1876 Edited by Edwin Elliott

23. Steam at Sheffield. From *Poetical Works* Vol 3 1835
- Brindley – the first canal builder

24. Holiday. From *Poetical Works* 1876 Edited by Edwin Elliott
- Maiden-hair. A fern

25. Sabbath. From *The Village Patriarch* book III

26. Wonders of the Lane. From *Poetical Works* Vol 3 1835
- titling – the hedgesparrow
- sunflower of spring – the dandelion

Sol - literary term for the sun
- firetuft – the goldcrest
- gloaming clock – a beetle which flies at dusk

27. The Excursion. From *Poetical Works* Vol 3 1835
- Fanny and Noe. – Elliott's daughters
- woodbine – honeysuckle

28. Air and Light on Stanedge. From *Poetical Works* Vol 3 1835
- enfranchised harvests – i.e. after Corn Law repeal

29. February. From *The Year of Seeds/ More Verse and Prose* Vol 1 1850

30. The Moors – Reflections. From *The Village Patriarch* book V

31. The Ranter. From *Poetical Works* Vol 3 1835

32. Epigram. From *More Verse and Prose* Vol 1 1850

33. Religion. From *More Verse and Prose* Vol 1 1850

34. Sonnet. Poet v Parson From *The Poetical Works of Ebenezer Elliott The Corn Law Rhymer* 1840
-Penn, Barclay, Clarkson. Quaker lay preachers noted for their oratory. Penn was the founder of Pennsylvania

35. Hymn. Written for the Printers of Sheffield. From *Poetical Works* Vol 2 1834

36. Hymn written for the Rotherham Political Union. From *Poetical Works* 1876
- Political unions were formed in most major towns in 1830/31 with artisan as well as middle class Membership to support the cause of Parliamentary reform.
-Brougham, Russell , Grey. Whig Politicians who played major roles in drafting and passing the 1832 Parliamentary Reform Bills.

37. The Revolution of 1832. From *The Corn Law Rhymes*

38. The Peoples Anthem. From *More Verse and Prose* Vol 1 1850

39. Prayer. From Ballad of Tom and Bet / *More Verse and Prose* Vol 1 1850

40. Sonnet: On a Pair of Spectacles. From *More Verse and Prose* Vol 1 1850

41. Dreams. From *The Village Patriarch* book VI Poetic tropes. Metaphorical use of words

42. A Poet's Epitaph From *Poetical Works* 1876 Edited by Edwin Elliott

Recommended Reading

Keith Morris and Ray Hearne. Corn Law Rhymer and Poet of the Poor. Rotherwood Press, 2002

Asa Briggs. Ebenezer Elliott. Cambridge Journal, August 1950

J. B Hobman. Ebenezer Elliot. Corn Law Rhymer. Contemporary Review. November 1949

Thomas Carlyle. Corn Law Rhymes. Edinburgh Review 1831. Reprinted in Miscellaneous and Critical Essays / Volume 3

Acknowledgements

The biographical information was obtained from a variety of contemporary sources and I thank the staff of Sheffield and Rotherham Local Studies Library for their help in making this available to me. The principal biographical sources were:

John Watkins. Ebenezer Elliott. Life Poetry and Letters 1850 [containing a reprint of Elliott's autobiographical memoir originally published in The Atheneaum].

January Searle [pseudonym for G. S. Phillips] Ebenezer Elliott. Life Character and Genius 1850.

Ebenezer Elliott. Commonplace Book 1841 - 1849 Edited by George Seary.

I am indebted to Keith Chandler for bringing to my notice the passage from Edward Dowden, quoted in his unpublished MA Thesis [Sheffield 1984]

Thanks too to Ray Hearne whose enthusiasm and inspired readings of Elliott's poetry rekindled my earlier interest in Elliott's writings.

www.ingramcontent.com/pod-product-compliance
Lightning Source LLC
Chambersburg PA
CBHW071915070526
44583CB00016B/1996